# THE IRISH-AMERICAN EXPERIENCE

# COMING TO AMERICA
## THE IRISH-AMERICAN EXPERIENCE

## BY SEAMUS CAVAN

Consultant:
James Shenton,
Professor of History,
Columbia University

Coming to America
The Millbrook Press
Brookfield, Connecticut

Cover photo courtesy of Culver Pictures

Map by Joe LeMonnier

Photos courtesy of: National Library of Ireland, Dublin: p. 11;
The Bettmann Archive: pp. 15, 21, 32, 57; Superstock: p. 16;
Art Resource: p. 22; New York Public Library Picture Collec-
tion: p. 26; Museum of the City of New York: pp. 28, 39, 50;
Culver Pictures: pp. 34, 40, 55; Boston Public Library: p. 42;
Life Pictures: p. 49; Photo Researchers (© George E. Jones III): p. 52;
University of Notre Dame: p. 58.

Library of Congress Cataloging-in-Publication Data
Cavan, Seamus.
The Irish-American experience / by Seamus Cavan ; consultant,
James Shenton.
p.   cm.—(Coming to America)
Includes bibliographical references and index.
Summary: Traces the history of Irish immigration to the United
States, discussing why the Irish emigrated, their problems in a
new land, and their contributions to American culture.
ISBN 1-56294-218-2 (lib. bdg.)
1. Irish Americans—History—Juvenile literature.   [1. Irish
Americans—History.]   I. Shenton, James Patrick, 1925-.
II. Title.   III. Series.
E184.16C38   1993   973'.049162—dc20   92-7512   CIP   AC

Published by The Millbrook Press
2 Old New Milford Road
Brookfield, Connecticut 06804

# CONTENTS

# INTRODUCTION

"The blood of all the world's peoples flows in the veins of Americans," the author Herman Melville wrote more than a century ago. "A vast ingathering from every continent, Americans have shared the common denominator of being, in most instances, either immigrants or the descendants of immigrants."

In our time, no less than in Melville's, the United States is a nation of immigrants. Each year, several million people pull up stakes and come to America, most of them in search of a new home. On the streets of American cities, it is common to hear Polish, Korean, Chinese, Italian, Spanish, and scores of other languages.

Like a great magnet, the United States has drawn people whose lives in other places have been filled with misery. Near-landless peasants of Europe, Latin America, and Asia, oppressed Jews of Eastern Europe, and political outcasts from dictatorships all over the world have fled their homelands for the United States. "The people I knew believed that America was the last place in the world where we could find freedom," said a recent refugee from Czechoslovakia.

Here in America, people have often overcome their ethnic differences. This has been true since the very beginning of our national history. "I could point out to you," wrote the French immigrant St. John de Crèvecoeur in 1782, "a man whose grandfather was an Englishman, whose wife was Dutch, whose son married a French woman, and whose present four sons have now four wives of different nations."

The story of American immigration has unfortunate chapters as well. Most ancestors of African Americans, for instance, came to the United States not bound for freedom, but bound by chains and condemned to the horrors of slavery. Nearly every immigrant has encountered discrimination, prejudice, and, all too frequently, outright violence. Sometimes the laws of the United States supported this discrimination. For a long while, people from Asia were turned away from American shores, and refugees from tyranny were sent back to their homelands.

This book is about the Irish Americans. In the 1840s and 1850s Ireland was struck by one of the greatest calamities in human history, the Potato Famine. During a space of five years over a million people either starved to death or died of disease. Another million, horrified and desperate, left Ireland altogether. Most of them came to America.

# THE SILENT LAND | 1

During the first week of June 1846 the farmers in County Cork, in southern Ireland, noticed that something was wrong with their potato plants. The stalks and leaves were covered with brown and black spots, and when touched, the stalks snapped like kindling. The farmers dug into the ground and found mostly black and mushy potatoes that broke apart in their hands and smelled horrible. The few potatoes that still seemed edible were tiny, much smaller than the hearty, healthy vegetables the Irish were used to harvesting.

The farmers in County Cork were scared by what they saw. If the potato crop failed, the people of Ireland would starve.

In 1845, the year before, the worst had nearly happened. Half of Ireland's potato crop had been destroyed by potato blight, a severe disease that attacks and kills plants. Ever since, the Irish had been hoping and praying for a healthy crop. It was not to be. Seeing the spotted stalks and the blackened potatoes, the farmers knew that the blight had returned.

The summer of 1846 was terrifying. It rains a lot in Ireland, but in June and July of that year it rained more than anyone could remember. In most places, the mornings were sunny and warm. But in the afternoons, huge clouds rolled in and settled low over the countryside, like fog. The temperature sometimes dropped thirty degrees, and rain fell for hours.

The birds stopped singing when the clouds rolled in. The cows stood silent; the sheep huddled together for safety; and the pigs stopped grunting. A strange silence fell over the land. At night, when the wind finally carried the clouds away, they left behind a light frost, like a dusting of snow, on the stalks of the potato plants. The Irish soon gave a name to the strange clouds: the "potato fog."

By the end of July, horrifying reports had come from all over the island—from the northern province of Ulster, from the eastern province of Leinster, from the southern province of Munster, and from the western province of Connacht. Everywhere the news was the same: The potatoes were rotting in the rain-soaked fields, sending up a foul stench of death and decay.

The newspapers told a grim story. "Where no disease was apparent a few days ago, all now is black," read one report. "The failure this year is universal," said a second. "For miles a person may proceed in any direction, without perceiving an exception to the universal destruction."

The destruction of the potato crop was a catastrophe for the Irish, the poorest people in Europe. Their diet consisted of potatoes.

Over eight million people lived in Ireland in the 1840s, most of them Roman Catholic. The reason they were so poor was that they owned so little land. For nearly seven hundred years they had been ruled by the English, who, after the 1500s, were Protestants. The English regarded the Irish Catholics as inferior beings who deserved to be subjugated, or kept down. Over the years, English armies had forced the Irish off

A family with seven children has been evicted. The door of their cottage has been boarded up to keep them from returning.

Irish lands. The vacated lands were then given to Protestants and settlers from England and Scotland.

By 1800 the Catholics owned just five percent of the land suitable for farming. Most Catholics owned no land at all. They lived in crude thatched cottages on huge estates owned by English landlords. The Catholics paid the landlords rent for the cottages and for the small plots of land on which they raised their food. Some of their rent was paid in money. The rest was paid in labor. The landlords used the Irish Catholics to grow oats, wheat, and barley and to raise pigs, cattle, and sheep. The Irish raised these crops and livestock but were not allowed to eat them. Virtually all the grain and meat was shipped across the Irish Sea to England.

What the Irish were left with was the potato. On the few acres of land they were allowed to have for themselves, the Irish grew the one crop that could feed their growing numbers.

The potato, unlike the crops the Irish grew for their landlords, required little work to plant or harvest. It grew well in most soils and under a variety of weather conditions. A tremendous number of potatoes could be grown on a small plot of land. For the poor Catholics of Ireland, potatoes and buttermilk were about the only foods they would ever eat.

For the Irish, the failure of the potato crop could mean only one thing—starvation. While the English continued to ship grain and meat from Ireland to England, hundreds of thousands of Irish starved to death. Hundreds of thousands more died from diseases that occurred because of the famine. Thousands wandered the roads in rags, thin as skeletons, desperately searching for food. There were soon too many dead to be buried; wolves and dogs fed on the corpses.

For many months, the English refused to do anything to help the Irish. At last, they agreed to set up "kitchens" where free soup would be given to the starving people. The soup was little more than hot water and provided almost no nutrition.

In Dublin, the largest city in Ireland, rich Protestants paid money to watch poor Catholics eat at the soup kitchens, like people watching monkeys feed at the zoo.

Visitors to Ireland were appalled by the horrors they found there. They described entire families huddled in fear and hunger, too weak to move. Wide-eyed children, their skin made nearly transparent by starvation, clung to the dead bodies of their parents.

Then, if possible, things got even worse. The landlords decided to use the land formerly planted with potatoes and grain for raising animals, whose meat could be sold at a good price in England. Countless Irish were evicted. Their thatched cottages and huts were torn down to prevent them from returning. Cruelly, the landlords sometimes paid their desperate, starving tenants a few shillings to pull down their own house. The sight of an evicted family sleeping in a ditch or by a hedge along a road became commonplace. Those who still had some strength built "scalpeens" for their families to live in. A scalpeen was built by leaning the beams from a destroyed cottage against a wall or hedge and covering them with thatch saved from the cottage's roof.

For the Irish, there seemed to be only one means of escape, but for many it seemed a solution almost as bad as death. They could leave, for America.

# the famine

A woman who as a young girl had lived in Ireland during the famine recalled the sense of "approaching death."

*I can recollect being awakened in the early morning by a strange noise, like the croaking or chattering of many birds. Some of the voices were hoarse and almost extinguished by the faintness of famine; and on looking out of the window I recollect seeing the garden and the field in front of the house completely darkened by a population of men, women and children, squatting in rags; uncovered skeleton limbs protruding everywhere from their wretched clothing, and clamorous though faint voices uplifted for food in pathetic remonstrance against the inevitable delay in providing what was given them from the house every morning. I recollect too, when walking through the lanes and villages, the strange morbid famine smell in the air, the sign of approaching death, even in those who were still dragging out a wretched existence.* [1]

A traveler through Ireland during the famine wrote of the horrors of death and starvation:

*We saw sights that will never wholly leave the eyes that beheld them, cowering wretches almost naked in the savage weather, prowling in turnip fields, and endeavouring to grub up roots which had been left, but running to hide as the mailcoach rolled by; groups and families, sitting or wandering on the highroad, with failing steps, and dim, patient eyes, gazing hopelessly into*

# THE EMERALD ISLE | 2

Ireland is one of the most beautiful countries in the world. From a distance, it looks like a brilliant green stone shining in the Atlantic Ocean, which is why it is often called the Emerald Isle. The central part of the country consists mainly of flat grasslands that are ideal for grazing cattle and sheep. Ireland is also famous for the fine quality of its racehorses, which graze on the abundant grass. Relatively low mountains can be found near each of the coasts. In general, the part of the country west of the River Shannon is much more rugged than the rest of the island, but it also features some of Ireland's most spectacular scenery. The largest and most important cities are Dublin, Cork, Galway, Limerick, Waterford, and Belfast, which is in Ulster.

Ireland was first settled by the Gaels. They came to Ireland about 2,300 years ago. The Gaels were Celts, the name given to a number of ancient peoples from central Europe who spoke related languages and shared a common culture. In Ireland, the Gaels built huge stone forts on the coasts. The walls of some of these forts enclosed more than forty acres. Inside were

Iveragh Peninsula, Ring of Kerry, on the southwest coast of Ireland.

SCOTLAND

*North Channel*

IRELAND

0            40 Miles

0            60 Kilometers

ATLANTIC
OCEAN

DONEGAL

NORTHERN
IRELAND

*Lough
Neagh*

ULSTER

Belfast

*Donegal Bay*

LEITRIM

MONAGHAN

SLIGO

CAVAN

LOUTH

*IRISH
SEA*

MAYO

*Clew Bay*

ROSCOMMON

CONNACHT

LONGFORD

MEATH

GALWAY

WESTMEATH

DUBLIN

Galway

*Shannon R.*

OFFALY

Dublin

*Galway Bay*

KILDARE

LEINSTER

CLARE

LAOIS

WICKLOW

*Mal Bay*

Limerick

*Barrow R.*

KILKENNY

CARLOW

LIMERICK

TIPPERARY

WEXFORD

KERRY

MUNSTER

*Dingle Bay*

CORK

WATERFORD

Waterford

Cork

*St. George's Channel*

Skibbereen

entire villages and farms. Gaelic society was divided into tribes and clans ruled by chiefs and kings. Most of the Gaels in Ireland were herdsmen, and wealth was measured by the number of cows a person owned.

The Gaels worshipped a large number of gods and believed that various animals and even rivers and trees had spiritual power. Their priests, called *druids*, possessed great power and influence in Gaelic society. Remnants of the Gaelic religion survive in Ireland in the form of folktales about leprechauns, banshees, pixies, fairies, and pookas. (A pooka is a mischievous spirit, usually harmless, that takes the form of an animal like a donkey or a rabbit. Often, a pooka has mysterious powers. A pooka in the form of a donkey, for example, might walk on its hind legs like a human and speak English.)

Poets were also revered members of Gaelic society. Because Gaelic was not yet a written language, poetry was memorized and recited. It often concerned the battles and other epic feats of legendary heroes from the past. Poetry was even believed to have magical power. The Gaels thought that by making fun of someone in a poem, a poet could bring misfortune and perhaps death upon that person.

This belief in the power, importance, and beauty of the spoken word has characterized Irish society to the present day. Ireland is often referred to as the land of poets. Gaelic, the language the Gaels brought to Ireland, is one of the oldest living languages in the Western world.

**St. Patrick** ▪ Sometime in the fifth century, probably around the year 432, the man known to history as Saint Patrick returned to Ireland. Patrick had grown up in the western part of Britain, probably near the present-day city of Bristol. When he was sixteen years old, he was captured and carried off by Irish marauders, and he spent the next six years as an enslaved shepherd in County Antrim, in northeast Ireland. During that time, he was sustained by his great faith. "Every day was spent in frequent prayer," he wrote later.

At the age of twenty-three, he escaped and returned to England and his family. One night he dreamed that a mysterious stranger named Victoricus came up to him and handed him a letter. As Patrick read the letter, he heard the "voice of the Irish." They said to him, "We ask thee, boy, come and walk among us once more."

Patrick understood the dream to mean that he should go back to Ireland and convert the Irish to Christianity. Upon his return, he established the Irish Catholic church at Armagh and traveled the countryside teaching the Christian religion. He "baptized thousands, ordained clerics everywhere, and gave presents to kings," according to his autobiography. Within a short time the Irish had embraced the faith that would become one of the foundations of their culture.

Saint Patrick is the most well-known figure in Irish history. According to legend, he rid Ireland of all its snakes. The shamrock, a tiny, three-leaved plant, became the national symbol of Ireland because Saint Patrick used it to explain the Catholic idea of the Trinity—the Father, Son, and Holy Spirit—to a powerful Irish king. Saint Patrick is believed to have died on March 17, possibly in the year 461. That date, St. Patrick's Day, is a national holiday in Ireland. In the United States it is celebrated, usually with a parade, in cities where large numbers of emigrants from Ireland have settled.

The authority of the Gaelic druids and poets was now taken up by Ireland's monks and missionaries. Irish priests traveled all over Europe teaching Catholicism. In Ireland, monasteries were built on the former sites of the Gaels' fortresses and were much respected centers of learning and culture. There, monks labored for many years creating illuminated manuscripts, the handwritten, beautifully illustrated versions of the Gospel and other sacred books. The

Saint Patrick, the patron saint of Ireland, converted the Gaels to Christianity.

The Virgin and
Child from the
*Book of Kells*,
the most famous
sacred text of the
eighth century.

most famous of these is the *Book of Kells*, which dates from the eighth century. The *Book of Kells* contains the oldest European representation of the Virgin Mother and the Christ Child.

*The English Conquest* ▪ In the early ninth century, seagoing warriors from Scandinavia began to raid Ireland's shores. These were the Vikings, the world's best shipbuilders and perhaps its fiercest warriors. The Vikings destroyed many of Ireland's monasteries and churches and established their own kingdom in Leinster. Dublin, Ireland's largest city, was founded about 830 as a Viking settlement. The famous Irish stone crosses, which feature a circle around a crossbar, date from the time of the Viking invasions.

These invasions forced the Irish to band together. Previously, Ireland had been divided into a number of different kingdoms. But then they united under the great king Brian Boru—the first and only king of Ireland—and fought off the Vikings.

Soon, another group of invaders came to Ireland, and they would prove much harder to defeat than the Vikings. In 1155, Pope Adrian IV, the head of the Roman Catholic Church, awarded Ireland to King Henry II of England. For the next several centuries, the English gradually increased their control over Ireland, beginning with Dublin and its surroundings and working inward.

The Irish were greatly angered by these limits on their freedom. They made many attempts to rebel against the English and regain their independence, but these uprisings only caused the English to clamp down even harder.

England started exercising greater authority over Ireland during the time of King Henry VIII, who ruled from 1509 to 1547 as England's first Protestant monarch. In 1541, Henry had the English and Irish parliaments, the lawmaking bodies of both countries, declare him "king of Ireland." Using this new authority, Henry and his successors steadily tightened their grip on Ireland and its Church. In 1560, for instance, it became illegal to say the Catholic mass in Ireland.

During the reign of Elizabeth I, from 1558 to 1603, English armies gained military control of Ireland. In the process, the armies suppressed the Irish who got in their way. When, in the 1580s, the Irish in the province of Munster rebelled, English troops laid waste to whole stretches of countryside. When the armies were done, wrote the English poet Edmund Spenser, "a most populous and plentiful country was left void of man and beast."

By the early 1700s, the English had made it virtually a crime to be Irish in Ireland. The Irish were not supposed to speak their own language, practice their own religion, or live on their own land. Between 1702 and 1715, the British Parliament enacted a series of incredibly harsh measures known as the Penal Laws. Under their terms, over a million acres of land were taken from Irish Catholics. Catholics were denied the right to vote and were barred from holding public office. Catholic bishops were forced out of the country, and religious orders were banished. Catholics were not allowed to teach at Irish universities nor could they become lawyers or judges. Furthermore, they were denied the right to operate their own schools.

But Ireland never gave in to England. The Irish resistance took many forms. Priests said secret masses in secluded fields, using large stones as altars. The people continued to speak Gaelic even though all official documents were written in English. Schoolmasters gave lessons outdoors, away from the prying eyes of English officials and soldiers. *Shanachies*, or storytellers, kept Ireland's tradition of spoken folklore alive.

*Ireland and Daniel O'Connell* ▪ In the early 1800s, life in Ireland was as hard as ever. For Catholics, poverty and discrimination had become a way of life. In some ways, though, they had reason for hope. The most repressive anti-Irish laws were repealed, and Irish Catholics were now free to attend school, speak their own language, and practice their religion. If they owned a certain amount of property, they were even allowed to vote. And for the first time, a great political leader had arisen who spoke eloquently for the interests of the Irish peasants.

Daniel O'Connell was born in County Kerry in 1775. As a boy, he was sent to France to be educated. Later, when the laws that prevented the Irish from entering the professions were abolished, O'Connell became a lawyer. His real interest, however, was finding a peaceful way for the Irish to regain control of their country. O'Connell believed that England was too powerful to be defeated militarily and that too many Catholics would suffer as a result of armed rebellion. "No political change whatsoever is worth the shedding of a single drop of human blood," he said.

O'Connell's first campaign was for Catholic Emancipation, which meant that Catholics would be allowed to sit in the British Parliament. Without representation in Parliament, Catholics had no one to speak for their interests. O'Connell raised money for his campaign by creating what he called the Catholic rent, a voluntary donation of one penny a month. Most Catholics were eager to contribute.

In 1829, fearing an uprising, the English at last allowed Irish Catholics to sit in Parliament. Among the first Irish Catholic representatives was Daniel O'Connell. Although the English soon made it even more difficult for Irish Catholics to vote, Emancipation was a great victory for the Irish. O'Connell was now hailed as "the Liberator."

Daniel O'Connell spent his life fighting to bring political and legal rights to Irish Catholics, who called him the Liberator.

Within Ireland, especially among a new class of young, educated Irishmen, there was some impatience with O'Connell's methods. According to these men, Ireland's freedom could never be obtained through patience and legal and political methods. Armed rebellion was the only thing the English would understand. Some of the Catholic poor, from whom O'Connell had always drawn his greatest support, had begun to agree. "The law does nothing for us. . . . To whom should we address ourselves? Emancipation has done nothing for us. Mr. O'Connell and the rich Catholics go to Parliament. We die of starvation just the same," said a poor Irish farmer in the 1830s.

But by the middle of the 1840s, the greatest issue for most Irish was simple survival, not independence. Between 1845, when the potato crop first failed, and 1851, more than one million Irish died of starvation and disease. About a million more left the country to search for a better life in America.

To the Irish, the mass emigration of their people was a tragedy no less great than the famine, but to the English, both were a blessing. One of the few laws passed to aid the suffering Irish provided money for those who were willing to leave the country. One landlord, when asked what his reaction was to the large number of tenants dying on his estate, replied that he was "delighted to be rid of them."

# THE COFFIN SHIPS | 3

During the 1840s two kinds of death were common in Ireland. Hundreds of thousands of people were starving or dying of such diseases as scurvy, typhus, famine dropsy, or dysentery. Hundreds of thousands more were scraping together what little money they had to buy passage on a ship for America. To those who were left behind there seemed little difference between death and departure. Few of those who left for America, even those who arrived there safely and in good health, ever returned to Ireland. Parents putting their sons and daughters aboard a ship for the New World knew almost for sure that they would never see their children again. "In those days, people made very little difference between going to America and going to the grave," one Irishman remembered years later.

When large numbers of Irish began leaving their country in search of a better life in the New World, a custom called the American wake began. Once a young person had decided to leave for America, relatives and friends would be invited to the home of the emigrant's parents on the night before departure. On the night of the American wake, all the well-wishers

*The Battery,* by Samuel B. Waugh, where many European immigrants caught their first bewildered glimpse of America.

would gather in the poor cottage of the emigrant's family. If the family had any money, food, tobacco, and drinks would be shared while all the guests joined in conversation about what the emigrant would be likely to find in America. The conversation would continue all night long. The older people warned the emigrant to be careful and made him or her promise to always write. The friends exchanged excited speculations with the emigrant about the promised land of the New World. Everyone told stories—of the good times they had known together, or about others who had emigrated and found happiness in America, or simply some of the many folktales that every Irish peasant seemed to know.

At sunrise, it was time for the emigrant to leave. "The last embraces were terrible to see; but worse were the kissings and the claspings of the hands during the long minutes that remained," wrote Harriet Martineau, an Englishwoman who witnessed the sad ending of one American wake.

Most of those who left Ireland during and after the potato famine were young. Many were the unmarried oldest sons or daughters of a family that had put all its money together to send them to America. The hope was that in the United States the emigrant would be able to earn enough money to bring the rest of the family over. Many others were young husbands who hoped that in a couple of years they would be able to pay the fare of their wife and infant children.

To the poor people escaping Ireland, the United States seemed like heaven. There, everyone could vote. No one paid taxes to a Church to which they did not belong. There were millions of acres of unsettled land in the West where one would not have to pay rent to a foreign landlord. The United States was a democracy, a land that believed, as Thomas Jefferson had written in its Declaration of Independence, that "all men are created equal." Most of all, the Irish believed, America was a land where a man who was willing to work hard could find a job and get ahead.

Some got a little carried away with stories of the riches in the New World. It was said that there was a river in upstate New York so full of fish that if you boiled the water from it, you would have the taste of salmon in your tea. A newcomer to America who bent down to scoop a coin off the sidewalk would be advised not to "bother with that one. Come on to the heap."

To reach that heaven, the emigrants had first to go through hell. Because English law had for many years required that only English ships could call at Irish port cities, most ships for the New World departed from English cities, especially Liverpool. To get to Liverpool, Irish emigrants crowded onto the decks of cargo ships. The voyage to Liverpool took twenty-four to thirty-six hours, yet aboard most ships there was no place for the passengers to lie down or even sit. They were often packed together so tightly that there was no room to move. They were unsheltered from the rain, the sun, or the cold. Below deck, the same ships carried pigs and cattle from starving Ireland to prosperous England, where they would be slaughtered for their meat.

While families in Ireland cried over the departure of their loved ones, newspapers in England rejoiced over the exodus of Ireland's "surplus population." "They are going! They are going! The Irish are going with a vengeance!" read an article in the *London Times* about Irish emigration. The same article reported joyfully that in a short time there would be as few Irish left in Ireland as there were American Indians in New York City.

In Liverpool, the Irish boarded sailing ships for America. Most of these ships were bound for Philadelphia, New York City, or Boston. Few Irish emigrants could afford the price of a ticket aboard a passenger vessel. Instead, most bought spots in steerage aboard cargo vessels.

Steerage was the poorest accommodation available. Most times it consisted of nothing more than a wooden shelf, no

# At Sea

In 1847, Stephen de Vere, a landowner from County Limerick, Ireland, wanted to see for himself the condition of the ships carrying Irish emigrants to the United States. Traveling as a steerage passenger, he wrote of the horror he saw among the sick aboard ship:

*Before the emigrant has been a week at sea he is an altered man. How can it be otherwise? Hundreds of poor people, men, women, and children, of all ages, from the drivelling idiot of ninety to the babe just born, huddled together without light, without air, wallowing in filth and breathing a fetid atmosphere, sick in body, dispirited in heart, the fevered patients lying between the sound, in sleeping places so narrow as almost to deny them the power of indulging, by a change of position, the natural restlessness of the disease; by their agonised ravings disturbing those around, and predisposing them, through the effects of the imagination, to imbibe the contagion; living without food or medicine, except as administered by the hand of casual charity, dying without the voice of spiritual consolation, and buried in the deep without the rites of the church.* 3

larger than six feet long and three feet wide. Great numbers of these shelves were stacked one on top of the other in the hold of a ship, so that hundreds of emigrants could be crowded together in an extremely small space. Usually, there was no more than two feet of space between shelves, which meant that the emigrant could only lie down and not sit up. On most ships, steerage passengers were not allowed on deck. They spent the entire voyage crowded together in the dark hold, without access to fresh air or sunlight.

The voyage to America took from one to three months, depending on the weather and the winds. Since there were seldom adequate toilet facilities in the hold, it soon became a filthy, stinking place that bred disease. In such close quarters, with so many of the Irish weakened already from the hardship and poverty of their lives, these sicknesses spread rapidly and killed many. Hunger continued to be a problem, because passengers were given only about a pound of bread or biscuits to eat each day.

The conditions endured by Irish emigrants on their way to America soon became notorious. The ships taking them became known as "coffin ships," because the passengers had about as much room on their shelves as they would in their coffins and because so many of them died before they reached America. In 1847, which was one of the years of the heaviest Irish emigration to the United States, eleven percent of the Irish emigrants died aboard ship.

For those who survived the voyage, the ship's landing at a port in the New World was a time of mixed emotions. There was relief at fleeing the filthy hold, bewilderment at the questions they were asked by U.S. government officials, sorrow at having left their country behind, and excitement and fear about making their way in a new land. Soon, most would find that America was a much different place from what they had expected.

# POOR PADDY WORKS ON THE RAILROAD | 4

The immigrants who stepped off the coffin ships in the New World had never seen anything like the cities of New York, Boston, or Philadelphia. New York City, at mid-century, for example, was home to more than 500,000 people. No city in Ireland was even remotely close in size, and most of the Irish immigrants were country people anyway.

Those who were lucky when they stepped off the ship were met by a friend or a relative who had emigrated before them. Others had the names and addresses of people who would show them the ropes in this new country. Many, however, were on their own.

Their first task was to find a place to live. The docks were usually lined with people looking to rent out rooms in a boardinghouse or an apartment in a tenement building.

Few of these accommodations were very pleasant, however. Most Irish immigrants wound up living in tiny apartments crammed into ramshackle, decrepit buildings in the poorest sections of town. Often, these apartments were nothing more

Irish immigrants pose in front of a camera just before docking in New York City. Hope and pride are etched on their faces.

than a single small, unpainted room in a building several stories high. For heat there was a primitive stove. There was no running water. Here, an entire family would do all its living—sleeping, eating, and entertaining. Most of these apartments had no windows and no access to sunlight or fresh air. The only toilet facilities would be on the ground level, usually outside behind the building. The same was true of sinks and running water. The toilets and water would be shared by everyone in the building, sometimes several hundred people.

The Irish ghettoes in the cities of the northeastern United States were soon as notorious for their poverty and suffering as the villages of Ireland had been during the famine. The English novelist Charles Dickens was appalled by what he saw in the New York City neighborhood known as Five Points, an infamous Irish ghetto. He described it as "a kind of square of leprous houses, some of which are attainable only by crazy wooden stairs. . . . Here, too, are lanes and alleys, paved with mud knee-deep . . . ruined houses, open to the street, whence, through wide gaps in the walls, other ruins loom upon the eye . . . hideous tenements which take their name from robbery and murder; all is loathsome, drooping, and decayed here."

As horrible as conditions were in American cities, they were better than things at home. The Great Potato Famine lasted from 1845 until 1851. In the years that followed, mass starvation ended, but Ireland remained a desperately poor country without the means to support its people. In the late 1800s Irish farms and estates began using great machines to cultivate and harvest crops. This meant fewer jobs for farm workers. In other countries out-of-work farmhands moved to cities, where they got jobs in factories. But Ireland had little industry, so moving to the city was no answer.

Moving to America was. During the 1840s, the years of famine, over 900,000 Irish emigrated to the United States. From 1851 to 1920, another 3,300,000 came. More than half of these newcomers settled in the states of New York, Pennsylvania, Massachusetts, and Illinois—chiefly in New York City, Philadelphia, Boston, and Chicago. By 1900 there were more Irish in New York City than in Dublin.

Many of the immigrants from other countries who came to the United States after the Irish headed westward to the vast unsettled lands beyond the Mississippi River. But Irish Americans tended to stay in cities. The memory of their horrible experiences as farmers in Ireland helped keep them away from the land. Also, most arrived in the eastern United States so poor that they had no money to go any farther. Another reason was that in the cities they found others like themselves—poor Irish Catholics trying to make their way in a strange country. This would have been much less likely to happen on the farms and ranches of the West.

Even so, life was tough for the Irish in America's cities and towns. Jobs were hard to come by. Most women hired out as domestic servants, while men worked as unskilled laborers on construction projects. The work was backbreaking and dangerous. So many Irish died building the country's railroads that it was said there was "an Irishman buried under every tie." Others found work as miners or digging America's canals. None of these jobs paid enough for the Irish to find their way out of the ghetto.

Conditions in the Irish neighborhoods were horrible. Poverty, disease, and hunger were the norm. Tenement buildings were unsafe and were often swept by fires. The crowded and unsanitary living conditions bred disease, and such deadly illnesses as tuberculosis, cholera, and dysentery were always more commonly found in the Irish section than in other parts

# tenement life

During the 1860s, a private agency in New York City investigated the living conditions of recent immigrants from Ireland. Its report of life in the tenements contained graphic descriptions of poverty and disease:

*Passing from apartment to apartment, until we reached the upper garret, we found every place crowded with occupants, one room only 5½ by 9 feet, and a low ceiling, containing two adults and a daughter of twelve years, and the father working as a shoemaker in the room, while in the upper garret we found a couple of dark rooms kept by haggard crones [old women], who nightly supplied lodgings to twenty or thirty vagabonds and homeless persons. This wretched hiding-place of men, women, and girls, who in such places become more vicious and more wretched, had long been a hot-bed of typhus, seven of the lodgers having been sent to the fever hospital, while permanent residents on the lower floors had become infected with the same malady and died.*

*Through a narrow alley we enter a small courtyard which the lofty buildings in front keep in almost perpetual shade. Entering it from the street on a sunny day, the atmosphere seems like that of a well. . . .*

*We enter a room whose ceiling is blackened with smoke, and its walls discoloured with damp. In front, opening on a narrow area covered with green mould, two small windows, their tops scarcely level with the courtyard, afford at noonday a twilight illumination to the apartment. . . .*

Irish boys pose in Mullen's Alley, New York City, 1888.

*A door at the back of this room communicates with another which is entirely dark, and has but one opening. Both rooms together have an area of about 18 feet square, and these apartments are the home of six persons. The father of the family, a day labourer, is absent; the mother, a wrinkled crone at thirty, sits rocking in her arms an infant, whose pasty and pallid features tell that decay and death are usurping the place of health and life. Two older children are in the street. . . . A fourth child, emaciated as a skeleton . . . has reared its feeble frame on a rickety chair against the window and is striving to get a glimpse at the smiling heavens whose light is so seldom permitted to gladden its longing eyes.* 4

Harper's Weekly, an established literary magazine, often printed anti-Irish cartoons. The caption for this one read, "650 Paupers arrived at Boston in the Steamship *Nestoria*, April 15th, [1883], from Galway, Ireland, shipped by the British Government."

of a city. There was even a saying in America about never seeing a gray-haired Irishman. The average Irish immigrant lived to be just forty years old.

Hardship bred despair. Many Irish came to believe that no matter what they did, they would stay poor and downtrodden. The use of alcohol was very high in Irish neighborhoods, as was the rate of criminal behavior. In New York City during the 1850s, more than half the people arrested were Irish. Most of these arrests were for drunkenness and fighting. Police vehicles became known as "paddy wagons" because they carried so many Irish off to jail. (Paddy is a nickname for Patrick, which was probably the most common first name for Irish men. It was often used as a way of referring to the Irish in general, usually in derogatory fashion.)

The poverty, the sickness, and the crimes helped create a good deal of prejudice against the Irish in the United States. Non-Irish and non-Catholic Americans feared the new-comers. They seemed so different, so hard to understand. The sheer number of Irish immigrants frightened some Americans, too. They were afraid that somehow the United States would be overrun, that America would become Irish instead of the Irish becoming Americans. Some worried that the Irish would take all the jobs and leave "real Americans" out of work. But the fact was that most Irish were forced to take jobs that no one else wanted because they were too dangerous, too difficult, or paid too little.

Stereotypes about the Irish became commonplace. Cartoons in American newspapers commonly depicted "Paddy" as a hulking, brutish, unshaven, badly dressed fellow, shovel in hand, or as a drunken sot. The Irish kitchen maid became a stock figure on the American stage and in novels. "Bridget" or "Mary" was often portrayed as quick-witted and clever with her tongue, but foolish, fearful, and superstitious in the practice of her Catholic religion and herself often too fond of alcoholic drink. Most important, she was always a comic character, not someone to be taken seriously.

Such prejudice made it very hard for the Irish to get ahead. To make matters worse, the longer the Irish remained at the bottom of the economic ladder, the stronger such prejudice grew. During the nineteenth century, few groups in America had such a low prospect for economic advancement as the Irish.

# THE BALLOT BOX AND THE CHURCH | 5

For the millions of Irish immigrants to the United States during the nineteenth and early twentieth centuries, one great dream came true. In America they found freedom. People might treat them poorly, make fun of them, and discriminate against them, but there were no laws forbidding them to vote nor from practicing their religion. Irish Americans took full advantage of this freedom and came to play important roles in politics and in the affairs of the American Catholic Church.

*Democracy in Action* ▪ The Irish very quickly made their presence felt in big cities. By the late 1850s they were influencing politics in some of the neighborhoods in Boston and New York City. By the 1860s they were in control of Tammany Hall, the organization of the Democratic party in New York. By the 1870s they were beginning to elect members of the United States Congress. And, by the 1890s many large American cities—New York, Boston, Philadelphia, Buffalo, Chicago, and San Francisco—were governed by Irish-American politicians.

**The political career of the colorful James Michael Curley of Boston spanned five decades.**

There were several reasons why the Irish were so successful at politics. Most could read and write and were able to keep informed about issues through the newspapers. Their experience in Ireland had given them some familiarity with the concept of democracy, even when it was denied them. Leaders like Daniel O'Connell had taught them there was strength in numbers, a lesson they applied in America. The many years of agitation and rebellion against English rule had given them experience in organizing to achieve a political goal. After having fought to rule themselves in Ireland for so long, the Irish were not about to waste their chance when given an opportunity to vote in America. They united in joining the Democratic party, and on election day they turned out and voted in full force.

The Irish realized that by electing their own candidates to office, they would gain access to something very important— jobs. In those days, mayors and other city officials had the power to hire people to fill every position from police officers to street cleaners, from toll takers to zookeepers. And politicians took care of their friends and supporters. The relationship between Irish politicians and the voters was based on mutual loyalty. The voters elected officials and expected them to help the community by providing jobs. In return the politicians expected the votes to keep themselves in office.

This arrangement was attacked for being corrupt. It often was. Municipal funds were misspent. Officials accepted bribes and payoffs. Incompetent people found their way onto the city payroll.

But the politicians also helped terribly poor communities. A political boss found a way to pay for the funeral of a voter whose family could not afford one. He made sure that coal was delivered to the poorest residents of the neighborhood so that they could heat their rooms. He arranged for newly arrived immigrants to get jobs on city construction projects. He pulled strings down at the courthouse so that young men were not sent to jail for fights that had hurt nobody. He might prevent a landlord from evicting a poor widow and her children from their apartment.

In return, the Irish politician asked for votes and help at election time. City workers were also requested to contribute a small portion of their salaries to the boss. Most Irish Americans regarded it as a fair exchange.

One of the most famous Irish-American politicians was James Michael Curley of Boston, who was elected mayor four times, congressman twice, and governor of Massachusetts once. In Chicago, Richard J. Daley served as mayor from 1955 until his death in 1976. Called "the last of the big-time bosses," Daley controlled Chicago politics long after Irish politicians in other cities had faded from the scene.

For years Irish Americans also dominated the politics of New York. The best-known Irish New Yorker was Alfred E. Smith. Born on the Lower East Side of New York City in 1873, Al Smith, like most boys in his neighborhood, dropped out of school after the eighth grade. Smith went to work at the local fish market. Ambitious for a better life, he turned to politics. In New York, politics meant Tammany Hall and the Democratic party. Smith was a natural politician, and with the support of Tammany he rose quickly. As a member of the state assembly, he did not let his lack of formal education hold him back, and he soon became known as the best-informed man in the state capital. In 1918 he won election as governor of New York and began serving the first of four terms.

In 1928 the Democratic party nominated Smith as its presidential candidate. To the voters in large American cities, he was a hero. Like them, he had come up the hard way. Like them, he spoke less than perfect English. And, like many of them, he was a Roman Catholic. As he campaigned in the cities, crowds pressed in to see him wave his famous brown derby and bands joyfully played his theme song, "The Sidewalks of New York."

# Getting Started in Politics

Tammany Hall, the organization of the Democratic party in New York City, was the most famous of all American political machines. It was also one of the most successful. For years its candidates won resounding victories at the polls. From the mid-1800s until the 1930s, New York City nearly always was run by a mayor and municipal government backed by Tammany. The organization drew its greatest support from the city's newcomers—recent immigrants who had become citizens and had registered to vote. For years, the majority of these voters were Irish. Not surprisingly, most Tammany leaders were Irish Americans.

George Washington Plunkitt described how as a young man he got started in Tammany politics:

*I set out when I cast my first vote to win fame and money in New York City politics. Did I offer my services to the district leader as a stump-speaker? Not much. The woods are full of speakers. Did I get up a book on municipal government and show it to the leader? I wasn't a fool. What I did was to get some marketable goods before goin' to the leaders. What do I mean*

It was a different story outside the cities. The United States was still a heavily Protestant nation, and Smith ran into a wall of prejudice. Protestants living in small towns and on farms were not ready to vote for a Catholic for president. On election day, Smith swept the cities, but it was not enough. He was overwhelmingly defeated.

*by marketable goods? Let me tell you: I had a cousin, a young man who didn't take any particular interest in politics. I went to him and said: "Tommy, I'm goin' to be a politician, and I want to get a followin'; can I count on you?" He said: "Sure, George." That's how I started in business. I got a marketable commodity—one vote. Then I went to the district leader and told him I could command two votes on election day, Tommy's and my own. He smiled on me and told me to go ahead. If I had offered him a speech or a bookful of learnin', he would have said, "Oh forget it!" . . .*

*I soon branched out. Two young men in the flat next to mine were school friends. I went to them, just as I went to Tommy, and they agreed to stand by me. Then I had a followin' of three voters and I began to get a bit chesty. Whenever I dropped into district headquarters, everybody shook hands with me, and the leader one day honored me by lightin' a match for my cigar. And so it went like a snowball rollin' down a hill. . . . Before long I had sixty men back of me, and formed the George Washington Plunkitt Association.* [5]

Thirty-two years later, in 1960, the Democratic party nominated another Irish Catholic for the presidency—John F. Kennedy. Born in Brookline, Massachusetts, in 1917, Kennedy was different from Al Smith. He had come up the easy way. Although his father, Joseph P. Kennedy, had faced his share of anti-Irish prejudice, it had not prevented him from earning a great fortune. By the 1920s, Joseph Kennedy was one of the wealthiest men in the United States. Young Jack Kennedy was educated in private schools and at Harvard University. When he entered politics in 1946, his father paid the bills for his campaign.

As a member of Congress from 1947 until 1953, and as a United States senator from 1953 until 1960, Kennedy made a profound impression. Handsome, intelligent, an eloquent speaker, he quickly moved to the front ranks of the Democratic party. In his campaign for president in 1960, Kennedy confronted head-on the belief that a Catholic should not be president. He said that if all American Catholics "lost their chance of being president on the day they were baptized, then it is the whole nation that will be the loser in the eyes of Catholics and non-Catholics around the world. . . ." On election day, Kennedy won a narrow but thrilling triumph.

Kennedy's election meant a great deal to Irish Americans. "I regret my father died before John Fitzgerald Kennedy was elected president because he had his heart broken when Alfred E. Smith was beaten," wrote the journalist Jimmy Cannon. "My old man felt betrayed by his country and went to his grave believing no man who was an Irish Catholic could ever be president."

Kennedy was part of a new generation of Irish-American politicians. By 1960 the day of the old-time big-city bosses was nearly done. Today, Irish Americans are more prominent in state and national politics than in local affairs. John W. McCormack and Thomas P. O'Neill, both Democrats from Massachusetts, have served as Speaker of the House of Representatives. Both Edmund G. Brown and his son, Jerry Brown, have twice been elected governor of California. President Kennedy's youngest brother, Edward M. Kennedy, was elected a United States senator in 1962 and rapidly became a leading figure in Congress.

John F. Kennedy's election in 1960 as the 35th president of the United States was the culmination of more than a century of political activity by Irish Americans.

St. Patrick's Cathedral on Fifth Avenue in New York City stands as a monument to the power of the Catholic Church in the lives of Irish immigrants. The Church helped to bring the Irish together and to improve their lot in America.

*The Catholic Church* ▪ In the 1830s and 1840s the Catholic Church was small and not particularly powerful in the United States. That changed after the Irish began arriving in large numbers. Despite their poverty, the Irish built thousands of churches across the country. Many of these churches established schools, where many Irish sent their children to receive religious training as well as education in academic subjects.

The Irish Americans soon came to dominate the Catholic Church in America. Each year hundreds of trained priests came from Ireland to serve in American parishes. In 1875, John McCloskey, the son of Irish immigrants, was named by the Pope as the first American cardinal. By 1900 half the Catholic bishops in America were of Irish descent, and thirteen of the seventeen American cardinals had been of Irish ancestry.

Catholic priests and nuns were often the most important members of the Irish-American community. In addition to their spiritual duties, they were often teachers. Many of them tended to the sick at a time when most Irish could not afford medical care. They also served as social workers, seeing to it that the poorest members of the community received enough food and warm clothes to survive the winter. Priests and nuns collected money to send back to Ireland during times of great trouble there. Often, the first person a newly arrived Irish immigrant would contact was a priest, who would help him find a place to live and possibly a job.

Much had changed for the Irish. In Ireland, most lived on the land. In America, most lived in the cities. (By 1920, ninety percent of all Irish Americans lived in cities, and Irish Americans were twice as likely to live in cities as were other Americans. Even today, three quarters of all Irish Americans live in or around cities in the East.) In Ireland, most Irish farmed for their living. In America, many dug ditches, or mined coal, or raised buildings, or built railroads. In Ireland, the Irish were often treated as criminals in their own land. In America, the Irish enforced the law as policemen. In Ireland, the Irish were denied many basic civil rights. In America, they were elected mayors and ran cities.

But the importance of the Church to the Irish remained the same, in both Ireland and America. In America, it was the one institution that linked the life the Irish had known before with the new life they had made across the ocean.

# A Happy Ending | 6

Throughout most of the nineteenth century, the Irish remained stuck at the bottom of the economic ladder. With the exception of African Americans, they were the poorest group in American society. Gradually, however, life got better.

When the Irish found steady work, living conditions and family life improved. People could afford to move out of slums. Couples married and had children. These children had no memories of a life on the land in Ireland. The only homeland they had known was the United States. Slowly, the Irish in America became Irish Americans.

By the mid-twentieth century, they had achieved considerable economic success. Although many still lived in poor city neighborhoods, many more had moved to the suburbs, where they owned their own homes. Irish Americans could be found in virtually every occupation in the United States, and the outlook for their children and grandchildren was even better. The Irish talent for political organization showed itself in the way the Irish Americans took part in the labor movement. Labor unions are organizations of workers from a particular

High school students in New York City take part in a Saint Patrick's Day parade on March 17. They celebrate their ancestry with pride and joy.

industry, such as coal miners or steelworkers. Over the years unions have struggled to obtain higher salaries and better working conditions for their employees.

Some of the earliest heroes of the labor union movement were Irish Americans. These courageous individuals risked losing their jobs, going to jail, and even being killed in order to help the workers, many of whom were Irish Americans, who built this country's cities and railroads and mined its coal. Among the most famous are Martin Burke, who in 1861 helped start the first national organization of coal miners, and Mary "Mother" Jones, who moved around the country helping poor workers.

In recent history, members of the poorer groups in American society have often excelled in sports and entertainment. The Irish Americans were no exception, especially in the field of boxing. Paddy Ryan, an Irish immigrant, was the only boxer to ever win the heavyweight championship in his first fight. In 1882 he lost his title to John L. Sullivan. Sullivan, who was known by such colorful nicknames as the "Boston Strongboy" and the "Great John L.," was the most popular and well-known athlete of his day. The last heavyweight champion to fight with bare knuckles, he lost his crown in 1892 to another Irish American, "Gentleman" Jim Corbett. Irish boxers were so popular in the United States in the late nineteenth century that fighters of other nationalities often adopted Irish-sounding names.

Irish Americans also won fame as participants in America's national pastime—baseball. Countless Irish Americans have graced the diamonds, and the two greatest managers of the first half of the twentieth century were both Irish Americans. The fiery John McGraw, who was famous for his temper tantrums and his mastery of strategy, won ten pennants in thirty years as manager of the New York Giants. Cornelius

Irish-American
heavyweight
champion Paddy
Ryan.

McGillicuddy, who used the name Connie Mack, managed the Philadelphia Athletics for fifty years. During that time, he won more games—and lost more—than any manager in history. (McGraw came in second.) In 1937, McGraw and Mack became the first two managers elected to the Baseball Hall of Fame. Another Irish American, Joe McCarthy, won eight pennants as manager of the New York Yankees. In his twenty-four years in the major leagues, McCarthy, who also managed the Chicago Cubs and the Boston Red Sox, compiled the highest winning percentage of all time. He, too, was elected to the Baseball Hall of Fame.

In the first several decades of the twentieth century, theater was the dominant form of popular entertainment in the United States. No showman was more successful than the Irish American George M. Cohan, who wrote and directed many popular musical comedies. Cohan also composed hundreds of hit songs. Among them were the enduring classics "I'm a Yankee Doodle Dandy," "Give My Regards to Broadway," and "Over There," which became the theme song of the American troops sent to fight in Europe during World War I.

More serious dramatic entertainment was written by Eugene O'Neill, the winner of several Pulitzer Prizes and the Nobel Prize for literature. O'Neill is regarded by many as America's foremost playwright. His greatest play, *Long Day's Journey Into Night*, was not produced until 1956, three years after his death. The play deals with the tragic conflicts that divide an Irish-American family. Among them are the father's memories of the extreme poverty that he had known in Ireland, which led him to choose economic security at the expense of his artistic talent. O'Neill gave the family in the play the last name of Tyrone, after County Tyrone in Ulster, which is where his ancestors had lived.

There were many great writers among the Irish in America. The most famous was F. Scott Fitzgerald, whose novels

F. Scott Fitzgerald kicks up his heels with his wife, Zelda, and their daughter, Scottie. Novelist Fitzgerald came to embody the glamour of the Roaring Twenties. But extravagance and tragedy caused his life and career to fall apart, mirroring the downward spiral of the lives of his fictional characters.

and short stories about the American upper classes in the 1920s were both popular and well regarded by serious literary scholars. His greatest novel, *The Great Gatsby*, concerns the disappointments encountered by a young man in pursuit of the American dream. Other Irish-American writers include John O'Hara and James Farrell. The novelists William Kennedy and Mary Gordon are perhaps the best-known living Irish-American writers.

# the fighting irish

The University of Notre Dame in South Bend, Indiana, was founded in 1842. Owned and controlled by the Congregation of the Holy Cross of the Roman Catholic Church, Notre Dame has long had a reputation for excellence in education.

The university also has a reputation for excellence in football. Knute Rockne, who coached Notre Dame teams from 1918 to 1930, established the university as a football powerhouse. Nicknamed the "Fighting Irish," Notre Dame teams have won a greater percentage of their games than have those of any other college.

Knute Rockne with the 1924 Notre Dame football team.

Notre Dame has always had legions of devoted fans. The sportswriter Jimmy Cannon once described the appeal Notre Dame held for the Irish Americans in his New York City neighborhood during the 1920s:

*The Giants were the New Yorkers' team. The Yankees got the tourists because of Babe Ruth. . . . The Brooklyn Dodgers were a road club that crossed the bridge to play the Giants. We didn't regard them as a New York team but Notre Dame in South Bend, Indiana, was our college, although no one from our neighborhood ever went there.*

*Photographs of Rockne were pasted on gin-mill mirrors and pictures of the Notre Dame team were enshrined among the fighters and baseball players in the barroom galleries of sports. The Notre Dame team, in a way, became like the gold watches. They were proof the Irish were doing good.*

*I assumed that everyone who played for Notre Dame was Irish, and poor. It didn't seem to be a college like Harvard or Princeton or Yale. Doing good was to work steadily as a truck driver or a longshoreman.*

*In that neighborhood, where education meant graduating from grammar school, the Notre Dame players were the perfection of our kind. We hadn't a president yet, and Al Smith had been beaten because he was one of us. On our mean streets no bands played, and a pennant never waved when Notre Dame won. But we were as much a part of that distant university on the prairies as though we had a diploma to prove it.*[6]

New chapters in the story of the Irish in America are being written today. In the 1980s, Ireland's economy took a dramatic downturn and tens of thousands emigrated to the United States in search of a better life.

This new generation of immigrants is quite different from previous ones. Today's Irish immigrants are much more likely to arrive in the United States on an airplane than on a ship, and they are better-educated and better off than those who came because of the famine. Because of television and the long history of the Irish in this country, those planning to emigrate from Ireland have a much better idea of what to expect when they get here.

In some ways, though, today's Irish immigrants are not that different. Most settle first in the big cities of the East Coast, especially New York City. Most important, what they hope to find here has not changed. Today's Irish, in common with all immigrants, are looking for a better life for themselves and their children. As they look at the achievements of the millions of Irish Americans, they have every reason to believe they will find it.

# MORE ABOUT
# IRISH AMERICANS

Franck, Irene M. *The Irish-American Heritage.* New York: Facts on File, 1989.

Grant, Neil. *Ireland.* Englewood Cliffs, N.J.: Silver Burdett Press, 1989.

Johnson, James E. *Irish in America.* New York: Lerner Publications, 1991.

Nardo, Don. *Irish Potato Famine.* San Diego, Calif.: Lucent Books, 1990.

Watts, James. *The Irish Americans.* New York: Chelsea House Publishers, 1988.

# NOTES

1. Quoted in Cecil Woodham-Smith, *The Reason Why* (New York: Dutton, 1960), p. 112.
2. Quoted in Seamus Mac-Manus, *The Story of the Irish Race* (New York: Devin-Adair Co., 1944), p. 607.
3. From Terry Coleman, *Going to America* (New York: Anchor Books, 1973), p. 99.
4. From John Francis Maguire, *The Irish in America* (London, 1868).
5. From William L. Riordan, *Plunkitt of Tammany Hall* (New York: Dutton, 1963), pp. 14–16. Originally published 1905.
6. From Jack Cannon and Tom Cannon, eds., *Nobody Asked Me, but . . .: The World of Jimmy Cannon* (New York: Holt, Rinehart and Winston, 1978), p. 9.

# INDEX